Amongst other things an unsuccessful proposal for the 2012 Cultural Olympiad

Contents

London, 19 March 2009

Artists are being challenged to use the nation as a blank canvas and create twelve inspirational commissions, as part of the London 2012 Cultural Olympiad. Artists Taking the Lead will create twelve new works of art in each nation and region of the UK, inspired by the 2012 Games.

The £5.4 million project, Artists Taking the Lead, will award up to £500,000 for each of the twelve works in the most ambitious art prize on offer in the UK. It is being developed by Arts Council England, in partnership with London 2012 and the Arts Councils of Northern Ireland, Scotland and Wales. Each new work will reflect the UK's artistic vision and become a creative celebration of the London 2012 Games.

Successful artists, who can submit ideas in any art form, will see their works displayed in iconic and unexpected locations throughout the UK, whether a hillside, beach or public space. There will be nine commissions in England and a further three, one each, in Scotland, Wales and Northern Ireland.

Moira Sinclair, Executive Director of Arts Council England, London, said on behalf of the UK Arts Councils: 'The London 2012 bid was always about more than England's capital city and about more than sport. Artists Taking the Lead illustrates that bigger, bolder vision — of art inspiring people up and down the UK to celebrate the Games, of nurturing and developing our artistic talent, and of culture and creativity at the heart of our national life. We're excited to be laying down such a unique challenge to artists. We want them to look at their region and their connections with fresh eyes, to mark a moment in our histories in unexpected ways and places across the country, to surprise and delight the world with their extraordinary artistic vision.'

The twelve successful commissions will take part in a final unifying celebration before the opening of the London 2012 Olympic Games.

Birmingham, 17 January 2009

Gavin Wade sends the Artists the Eastside
Projects Requirements.

A.
We have joined together to execute functional
constructions and to alter or refurbish existing
structures as a means of surviving in a capitalist
economy.
B.
Eastside Projects is an artist-run space as public
gallery for the city of Birmingham and the world.
C.
Eastside Projects is a self-stabilising energy event
complex.
D.
Eastside Projects will ensure it is intrinsic to the
structure of the city and therefore necessarily
part of the sphere of public support through
government subsidy. This is correct and proper
as part of the fight to keep at bay the monopoly of
cultural homogeneity. The artist-run space is not a
stop-gap. The artist-run space is a public good.
E.
Eastside Projects is a not-for-profit organisation,
working in partnership with Birmingham City
University and revenue funded by Arts Council
England West Midlands.

F.

We will question the organisation's status and respond to the pressures towards becoming an institution.

G.

Eastside Projects will aim to commission and present experimental contemporary art practices and exhibitions and fully participate and support the cultural activity of the city both inside and out.

H.

Eastside Projects will locate and utilise radical historical positions.

I.

Eastside Projects will promote the idea of art and other spatial practices as important forms of alternative knowledge production. We will ensure the space and programme offer tools for the creation and comprehension of contemporary visual culture alongside the immediate context of forthcoming regeneration of Eastside.

J.

We will question the role and function of art within the urban environment.

K.

We will question the concept of a default setting.

L.

The gallery is to be not a standard but a model to be adapted and exploited.

Glasgow, 13 September 2010

Francis McKee explains how the Centre for Contemporary Arts flourishes.

I was made Interim Director at Glasgow's Centre for Contemporary Arts in 2006, whilst discussions were held between the organisation and its core funders. The CCA was founded in 1992, replacing the Third Eye Centre, an experimental arts organisation. The CCA was more focused on a visual arts and live arts programme. Awarded a major Lottery grant, it was refurbished and relaunched in 2001. The impressive new building promised much, but it was perhaps too upmarket and somehow out of sync with the bohemian art community audience that once inhabited it. The much larger facilities also encouraged a larger programme, though the programme funds had not increased in proportion. By late 2005, the CCA had run into large debts.

When I started, there was a debate with funders on whether there was a need to keep the CCA in a city that had acquired a large and sophisticated arts infrastructure. It was decided that the CCA would stay open, under the overall care of the Scottish Arts Council, while we experimented to see if it could re-establish a relevant role in the city and broader cultural community.

In a large building, then silent and inactive, it was clear that momentum had to be quickly established. Many organisations offered to take over the space, but that risked the loss of the unique contribution that the CCA, and before it Third Eye Centre, had made to Glasgow and the wider arts community. It also meant that the building could become closed to the public. We redefined our relationship with a number of cultural tenants and developed an open source policy for the whole building, asserting creative control over the selection of partners who we felt were proposing programme ideas that were a complement to our own programme and purpose.

This approach has had several clear benefits: it has facilitated the expression of other curatorial voices in the building; it has created a shared sense of ownership of the CCA; it has brought in a wider and more varied programme and new audiences. Sharing resources has enabled the CCA to provide in-kind support to other publicly funded arts organisations and cultural practitioners. This new way of working is enabling our staff (who are all employed on a part-time basis) to re-establish a core programme, co-ordinate a series of partnership programmes and provide a platform that supports a huge range of artists and organisations across the city.

Birmingham, 29 October 2011

A conversation between the Artists and
Gavin Wade on the occasion of Eastside Projects'
Public Evaluation Event.

   GAVIN
I'm going to ask the artists about their Eastside
Projects exhibition.
   TOM
Does your contemplation of the situation fuck with
the flow of circulation.
   JOANNE
That phrase felt like it identified a sort of shift
… When we started making the exhibition in
late 2008, it felt like a pivotal point and we
wanted to demonstrate an attitude that was an
acknowledgement of that. We wanted to force
a viewer to address their mind specifically as to
whether their contemplation of the situation was
fucking with the flow of circulation.
   GAVIN
I'd forgotten how it felt when you first sent the title
over. I read it in relation to the economic crisis.
The word circulation was about economics and the
flow of money and about who's in charge of that.
   TOM
The title was adapted from a sentence in a
Jan Verwoert text. He describes himself as a

circulating agent within this network or system of the artworld, as all artists and curators are of course. We were interested in that idea, but we took the phrase and worked with it so that maybe it became more like a riddle or a slogan.

JOANNE

We wanted to make it sound like a political kind of challenge. We wanted to highlight our own concerns about the political purpose of the art we make. Of course these things were of concern before the economic shift in 2008 … it's just that at that point in time there seemed a possibility of increased audibility. I'm not so sure now.

GAVIN

How would you describe the metamorphosis of form and content in your works from Eastside Projects to CCA to Fettes College?

JOANNE

It's very simple — the tunnel became a worm and it also became the cat and the boot. I don't mean to be facetious, but that's really how it happened. Sorry, I should probably try to explain myself better.

TOM

A description of the metamorphosis of form that you are asking would involve an account of how we work in the studio. We work with scraps of foam-board, paint and magic tape. We are not precious about the models we make and they often get re-used. A tunnel might well become something else. The loop of a worm might become the back of a cat, and so on.

JOANNE

The description of the metamorphosis of content would involve a detailed account of each particular context and how we came to be working in that context. Should we do that?

GAVIN

Can you summarise how you approached this space, Eastside Projects, and other galleries like CCA and non-galleries like Fettes College?

JOANNE

Is it possible to summarise how we approach a space? I don't know. Maybe the only thing that is always common to our approach is the process of working together.

TOM

When we are approached by a gallery or another organisation, we start by talking about that. We talk about how we feel about being approached, what we think of the organisation — such as what we think of their exhibition programme, that sort of thing.

JOANNE

I probably shouldn't say this, but often we talk first about the things we might not like about a space or an organisation. We focus on the negative. We try and pinpoint where the discomfort might be.

TOM

Our project at Fettes College developed in response to an opportunity to make a proposal for a public commission for the Edinburgh Art Festival. We started to talk about what we might propose, and we talked a lot about Edinburgh … its differences to Glasgow. We were interested in Edinburgh as the historic seat of power in Scotland and how this creates hierarchies of influence that manifest themselves within the city's cultural venues, its educational establishments and of course the architecture of the city itself.

JOANNE

We also spoke about the art festival. We were working with Collective and we felt we were unlikely to get the commission money … that it was too difficult to compete with proposals from larger venues like the Scottish Gallery of Modern Art and the Fruitmarket. We chose Fettes College as a site for the project because it seemed to offer an opportunity to coalesce these discomforts.

TOM

Obviously, this was a very different conversation to the one we had when you first approached us to do a project here at Eastside Projects Gavin. Eastside Projects wasn't predictable in its requirements and particularly at that point; it wasn't clear what it wanted from us. We'd often used motifs to create something iconic, monumental …

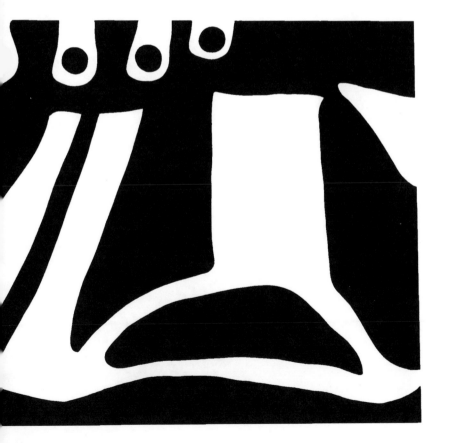

LATION OF THE SITUATION FUCK WITH THE FL

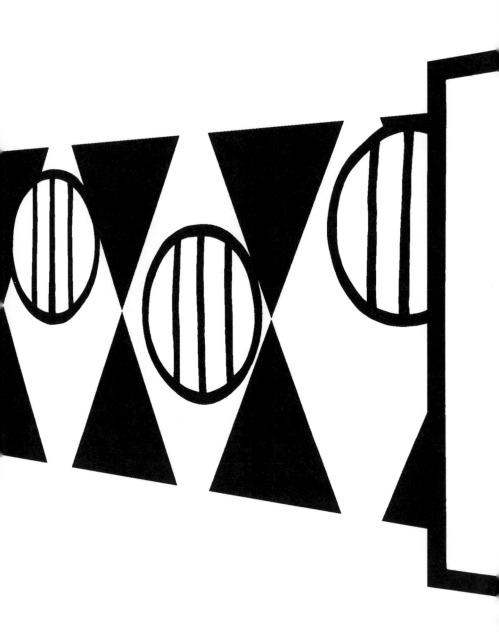

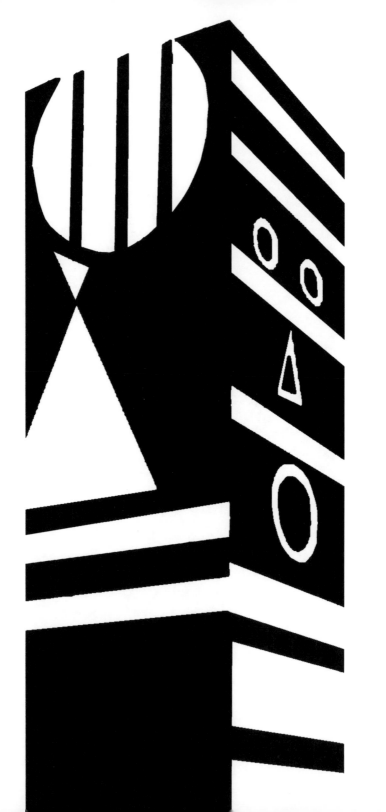

JOANNE (interrupting)
… as well as something to hide behind!
TOM
It became necessary to come up with some new strategies. We wanted to make a theatre for thinking …
JOANNE (interrupting)
The walk through the tunnel could be described as a participatory performance, but it was such a basic, everyday activity. The interaction was meant to take place in your head instead.
GAVIN
With other works you've made it's like coming face to face with some other consciousness, but with the tunnel, you were inside the consciousness!
JOANNE
It's just going into a patterned zigzag construction.
GAVIN
From the tunnel at Eastside Projects to the boot and cat at Fettes College there is a circulation of function as you present both expressions of being the invited and the host. How is this role of host a motivation for you as artists? Have you rationalised this role?
JOANNE
Actually the idea to have a gallery in the back leg of the cat came through a joke Tom made in the studio. We had already designed the boot so that

it could accommodate Elizabeth's film and having
something in the cat gave a sense of balance …
and the joke stuck. Positioning Chris's sculpture
within this space depended very much on Chris.
Not everyone would be prepared to exhibit in the
back leg of a cat. However, I'm not sure that this
demonstrates that we have rationalised our role
as hosts.

TOM

Our structures became another kind of institution
… an institution where another kind of knowledge
or way of knowing could be experienced!

JOANNE

At Fettes we were interested in creating a
conversation between a number of practices and
the context. So we invited Chris and Elizabeth.
The nature of the project at Fettes, how it came
about, meant we already had a role that is perhaps
more usually associated with that of a curator.
This was not so unusual for us; we often describe
our practice as one of curating our own work. The
idea to host work by Chris and Elizabeth within
our structures came, as is often the case, through
problems the context threw up. It became clear
that positioning work inside the Fettes college
building was going to be problematic. There were
issues of public access to consider.

TOM

It seems we require problems, although I couldn't
say we always enjoy that aspect of how we work.

JOANNE

The CCA offered its problems up to us before
we were even asked to exhibit there. You have
to understand, we'd had a long relationship with
the place, not just as artists in Glasgow, but also
working there … a situation like that, of personal
experiences rubbing up against the wider
reaching shifts that were characterised by such
Lottery funded redevelopment — well, there was
a lot to negotiate!

TOM

The worm emerged from an extended process of
intellectual and emotional digestion!

GAVIN

Does your work become part of place-making or
place-breaking?

TOM

Each situation has a different requirement.

JOANNE

Gavin, I appreciate your attempt to create an
internal rhyme — of course that appeals, but I find
both those terms unhelpful. I spend a great deal of
time dodging the smooth attractions of a rhetorical
dichotomy. In fact, and I feel very strongly about
this, I am continually irritated and frustrated at the

slippery exchange of one mode of meaning for another ... and when words enter the picture, this is a particular problem.

TOM

Joanne, do you mean that art is too readily, too easily, transcribed?

JOANNE

Yes, of course — but it's the reverse of this too, it's what happens in the process of making art and curating art, when written and spoken language arrives uninvited and inappropriately dressed. There are default modes of exchange. New orthodoxies of translation emerge dangerously quickly. There's a presumption of parity that is mistaken. Sitting here now, talking like this, it's a frustration, it's not simple. These words come out of my mouth, but you shouldn't trust them. Sometimes when I speak there's a buzzing in my head, it's a white noise, like a swarm of bees buzzing!

TOM

I get that too. There's the buzzing ... Of course this sounds ridiculous, but I think we are both trying to describe something important.

JOANNE

But the words don't follow on from one to the other, that's the important thing to say! There's incoherence, a garble, a garbled ... the letters get mixed up ...! Do you know what I'm saying?

It won't read from left to right. The buzzing is the sound that announces a fracture, a break … some sort of seizure, or a moment of violence. Nothing should be taken literally.

TOM

We believe all this very strongly, but you'll have to excuse our clumsiness … We walk with heavy feet for a reason. We may leave an impression that's the opposite of what we intended to say. I admit, its best to be cautious when it comes to words. Of course we work with them all the time … to make the work and within the work, but …

JOANNE (interrupting)

I'm sorry Gavin, we didn't really answer your question.

GAVIN

How would you approach Eastside Projects three years later? Is it possible to imagine an approach to this site in ten years, twenty years' time?

JOANNE

Is it already three years ago?

TOM

No, the project was in the summer of 2009 — but I suppose its three years since we first started talking about the project.

JOANNE

I don't know. Maybe we would draw direct attention to our absence.

GAVIN

We have been attempting to envision an Eastside Projects in 2021 and what the existing conditions would be then. What we would like them to be. Is it dangerous to imagine ideal conditions to work in?

JOANNE

It would be dangerous for me. I worry that when we talk about ideal conditions we imagine that we might have some kind of control over such circumstances. This may be naïve. I don't know Gavin, perhaps your experiences of Eastside — your experiences in your own life even, have led you to believe that you can engage in such a process, but I feel deeply suspicious. I can't help but consider this idea of envisioning as anything but detritus flung out from the tailspin of early twenty-first century business practices … Sorry, I'm speaking too personally. I don't know, I'm not sure, but perhaps there have been times when I felt I was working within ideal conditions, but on reflection, although conditions were good for me, they were certainly far from ideal for most.

TOM

Are you saying that you suspect that any artistic or cultural ideal may well be a distraction from more urgent matters? Does that mean we should be hesitant about imagining the future? I admit, I also feel uncertain as to the nature of ideal

conditions and if they could, or did exist who
would benefit from them …

JOANNE

… and would they be the ones who most needed
or deserved such conditions?

GAVIN

Does your contemplation of the framework of
institutions fuck with the efficiency of institutional
barriers?

TOM

Would an efficient institutional policing allow and
accommodate for its barriers to be fucked …?

JOANNE

Do you think that contemplating the framework of
the institution, as you say, we might come to this
understanding … an understanding that can result
in empowerment … I don't know, I'm not sure. I
don't think we would want to make that kind of
claim for what we do.

TOM

I don't know, I'm not sure. An institution that holds
and retains power and will not let its barriers down
and will not admit, or let others understand how
it holds on to that power … yes, these things do
make me angry.

GAVIN

You've said 'You can take it as a thing, or you
can take it as a thing.' Where does that leave the

person to thing relationship? I like this idea of in reality there may only be one way to approach a thing!

JOANNE

The title addresses the viewer directly so the viewer is directly involved in thinking about their relationship to the thing …

TOM

… and the situation the thing is in determines this thinking.

JOANNE

For us, with the work we make, the thing is always a problem — well, both a problem and a necessity. It's a necessary decoy — yes, of course, we need the things we make, to make the work we make.

TOM (interrupting)

… but these things we make, they also seem to be some kind of a block … they are stubborn and obstructive …

JOANNE (interrupting)

Or is it just that they provoke stubborn and obstructive behaviour in their viewers? I think the things are like a comfortable armchair.
You tell someone, 'don't sit here' and they nod in acknowledgement, only to take off their coat, drape it over the back and sink down into the soft cushions! It's the easiest place to be after all.

GAVIN

At what points have you been forced to admit that direct serious action is necessary? I like the idea that you are able to recognise the moment, the conditions that lead you to the conclusion that direct serious action is therefore necessary. When have you recognised it? When do you see others comprehending this moment of action?

TOM

Direct serious action was therefore necessary at the CCA in Glasgow in October 2010 and in the months leading up to it. It was appropriate in that particular time and place. We have not been forced to admit anything however, but perhaps you have Gavin.

GAVIN

As a gallery we are often having to prove The indirect exchange of uncertain value. As an artist-run space we want to deal with The indirect exchange of uncertain value. Does this phrase The indirect exchange of uncertain value outline the work of an artist? Your work?

TOM AND JOANNE (speaking together)

Yes.

TOM

Yes, this is how it feels for us to make art, of course. Most of the time, well, most of the time these conditions and exchanges are born out of generosity, despair, hope, resignation.

JOANNE

Of course, we are very interested in the idea
of value and art … and who has the power to
consolidate this value … the artist, the gallery, the
state …?

TOM (interrupting)

You can consolidate your debts, but for whose
benefit …?

JOANNE

Yes and even working with an organisation like
this, like Eastside Projects, for example — well,
what kind of exchange are we participating in
now? How thorough are the ethical arrangements
you have in place for the creative exchanges that
occur within Eastside Gavin?

TOM

I think Joanne is trying to ask you if this, is this an
indirect exchange of uncertain value?

GAVIN

What are the relationships between indirect
exchange, direct serious action and the flow of
circulation?

JOANNE

I don't know. I am trying to draw direct attention to
our absence.

TOM

I don't know, I'm not sure. I am trying to draw
direct attention to our absence.

Glasgow, 9 October 2009

A proposal for the 2012 Cultural Olympiad.

The proposed project will employ four distinctive sculptural motifs to create an artwork that occurs across Scotland, across a twelve month period. The artists have designed absurd yet familiar forms that will engage audiences at an annual calendar of events that includes gala days such as St. Monan's Sea Queen Day and fire festivals such as Burghead's Burning of the Clavie. The four sculptural forms will create a distinctive sight as they travel together to their host communities.

This existing calendar of events provides an opportunity to draw on a rich shared history of community participation. The artwork will visit local Highland Games as well as more unorthodox sporting events, such as the Kirkwall Ba' game and the Kelty coal race. The artwork will visit events that are home-grown, often idiosyncratic and usually occur without any commercial motivation. The project will thoroughly research the large number of potential host events and develop a programme that will represent all of Scotland's different audiences.

The first object is a large pyramid-shaped marquee featuring the artists' signature pink and black pattern and a cartoon face. The marquee will be used by communities as a refreshments tent; for bric-a-brac stalls; as a performance space or in any number of other ways. Many events are short of funds and as well as providing the marquee, we will provide financial and in-kind support. We want people to see the marquee as an opportunity to do something they might not otherwise be able to do and we will develop relationships with host communities that enable them to do this. It's a chance for people to be involved in a wider event that connects people and places across Scotland.

The marquee will create an iconic landmark at a host event, whether as a stand-alone feature or as one of a number of tents at a fairground. It will create a strong visual identity and enable visitors to create powerful and memorable images. Visitors will disseminate still and moving images, enabling the artwork to function for a collective nationwide audience.

The marquee, as with all the other objects, will be designed by the Artists, working with the Architect and be produced by specialist fabricators. It will be designed to enable easy siting and relocation. It will be erected by trained staff employed by the project and will retain staff onsite for the duration of each event.

The second object is a giant stickman that incorporates its means of transport into its construction and design. The kneeling stickman, a simple and recognisable form, will be incorporated onto a large flatbed trailer where it will remain as it travels between events. This will create a memorable and iconic image as it is towed in convoy across Scotland.

At host events the travelling sculptural motif will function as a parade float. It will be part of the processions and parades that are the focal point of many events, or will provide a new focus at events where these do not occur. The stickman float will provide a spectacle and create opportunities for participation at host events. Host communities will have the chance to be part of a parade, with the opportunity to take ownership of the stickman by decorating it and its float.

The willing involvement of host events is central to the success of the proposed artwork and the project will develop relationships with event organisers, communities and groups in the period leading up to 2012. We would develop trusting, co-operative relationships, selecting hosts who wished to be actively engaged in the project. We will provide hosts with the support to make their participation memorable and worthwhile. With the stickman float this means creating conversations with host communities as to how they may wish to use it and then providing them with the resources to facilitate this.

47

The Artists' third object is a mobile kiosk in the form of a pink and black diamond patterned cube. The kiosk will create an opportunity for event visitors to become active participants within the artwork. The kiosk will be a distribution point for small items and personal accessories decorated with the project motifs. These will have a use value that could enhance the host events. Diamond motif swimming caps would be distributed to Loony Dook swimmers. Children's sport equipment (sacks with faces for sack races) would be available for children's races. Decorated rain capes would be handed out at a wet Highland games. The items will become props or costumes that create compelling and humorous scenes.

The fourth element is a series of smaller scale objects conceived to facilitate the involvement of children. The objects utilise a familiar motif of a hand-drawn face and take the form of costumes and objects that initiate and encourage younger children's games and play. As with the recipients of items from the mobile kiosk, the children will become part of the performance of the artwork as they play and interact with the objects. We will explore the objects' potential to enable imaginative play and fun sporting activities, such as races and obstacle courses. We will design costumes that can be used by both children and adult facilitators.

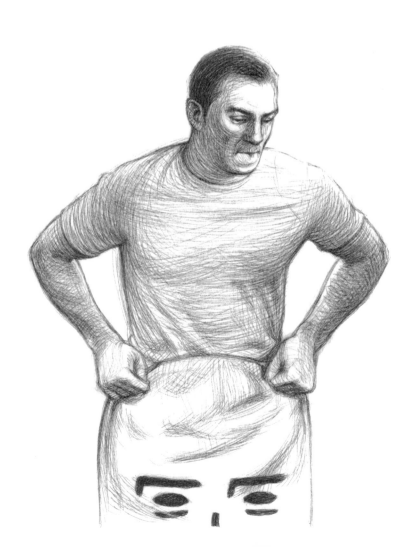

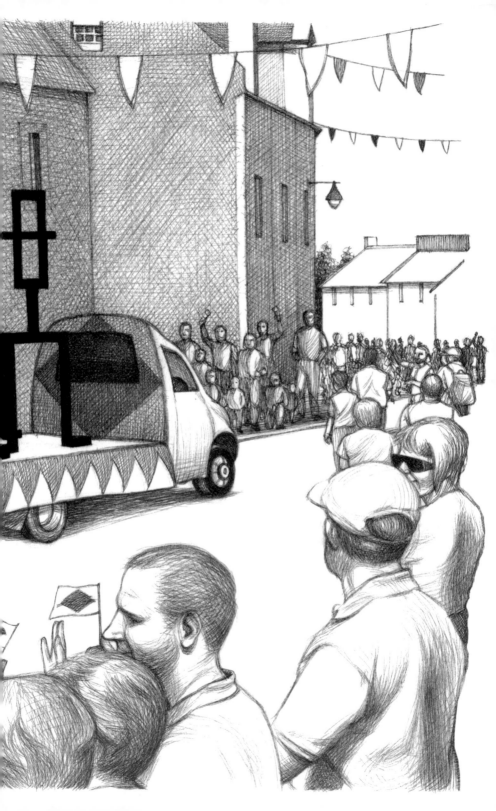

Some of the events we have been researching are already very focused around children and special children's events are a feature of many galas and games. The artwork will add value to these events and appeal to an important element of the core audience at the host site. At events that currently have no specific children's activities we will work with local groups, organisations and schools to develop something new. We will give children a valuable and memorable experience and encourage them to feel part of a nationwide event and the 2012 Olympics. The children's activities will be co-ordinated and supported by an appropriately experienced Children's Activities Facilitator.

At the end of 2012, the four objects will have activated locations and audiences across Scotland. We intend that the objects will continue this role and provide a valuable cultural legacy for the Cultural Olympiad and we propose to gift the four objects to an organisation that will be able to support their continued use.

ORGANISATIONAL STRUCTURE
The key delivery team working with the Artists on the project will be the Project Manager, the Consultant Producer and the Architect. The Project Manager will be responsible for the day-

to-day management and co-ordination of the project and will research and liaise with host communities, participating sites and events. The Consultant Producer will advise and oversee the project and also provide support and mentoring for the Project Manager. We will develop a responsible programme of Internships and Volunteering to support the core operations of the delivery team. The Intern(s) will receive mentoring from the Project Manager and gain valuable experience through their access to the organisational and creative development of the project.

The Architect will develop the design of the objects and co-ordinate and oversee their fabrication. The Artists will have overall responsibility for the creative vision and development of the project.

EVENT CO-ORDINATION AND DELIVERY
The objects will appear at twelve events throughout 2012 and will be on the road for three separate journeys during the year. Each of the three journeys will be approximately four weeks long and will each take in four events.

The three journeys of four weeks will be planned and co-ordinated to maximise geographical coverage of Scotland and will be split into the following three areas: west central and borders, east coast and Highlands and Islands. Each journey will be co-ordinated and planned so that objects travel from one event onto the next. In the periods when the objects are not on the road they will be parked securely, with the objects packed away into their transportation.

An event team of four people will be employed to travel to the twelve host sites and facilitate the project. This team will transport the objects and be responsible for siting and unpacking. The four team members will also facilitate the artwork, enable community activities and be responsible for general invigilation and health and safety. One of the team will have special responsibility for facilitating the children's activities.

CONCLUSION

Our project relates to the themes, relationships and juxtapositions found within Olympic host cities.

Our project will focus on and support local events that are inclusive and open to the whole community. Not all audiences welcome public art initiatives and some may consider some initiatives as top-down cultural imposition. We aim to produce a bottom-up event that can function for local communities and for wider national and international audiences. By working in partnership with host events, our project will produce a real and positive relationship between communities and the Cultural Olympiad project.

Our project reflects the three values of the Cultural Olympiad:

1.

Celebrating the UK and welcoming the world. Our project brings focus and support to the many local cultural and sporting community events that happen throughout the year in Scotland. The project will recognise these events as significant cultural activities and will represent and celebrate the diversity of contemporary Scotland. The project will allow and encourage visitors to the UK throughout the Olympic year to participate in Scotland's existing cultural activities.

2.

Generating a positive legacy. Our project will be a celebration and invigoration of community events across Scotland. It will recognise the on-going traditions of these community activities and support their role in generating social cohesion and sustaining the quality of community life. The objects will be gifted to an organisation that will enable their continued use.

3.

Inspiring and involving young people. The project has been conceived to inspire and involve communities and the objects have been designed to facilitate this. We will develop relationships that encourage and support young people to take part as active participants. Our project includes an element designed to specifically appeal to and involve children. We will facilitate children's involvement at events where there are currently no activities for them. At events where children's activities do already take place, we will ensure that children are welcomed into the wider project. The artwork offers an opportunity for the individuals, groups, families, schools and children that make up communities to be involved together.

Edinburgh, 30 March 2011

The minutes of a steering group meeting at Fettes College.

PRESENT
Debi, Jack, Barbara, Vanessa, Gemma, Kate, Geraldine, Elaine, Callum, Tom, Anne, Joanne.

APOLOGIES
Pauline, Emlyn, Edwin.

Previous Minutes approved. No Matters Arising.

OUTLINE
Tom and Joanne presented models of the works to be sited at Fettes College. They showed the group models of a giant cat and a giant boot in front of a scale model of Fettes' front arches. Chris' work will be displayed in the back leg of the cat and Elizabeth's work will be screened in the toe of the boot.

There will be an information board, posters and a manned station at the main entrance to Fettes for the four weeks of August. The two weeks after may be opened up for school visits or invited groups.

Tom and Joanne discussed what might happen to the structures after the project had finished. There are discussions with the Contemporary Art

Society about the possibility of the works being given to a public gallery.

It was suggested that possibly there could be an exhibition of the posters and documentation of the project, possibly at Fet-Lor youth club after the end of the project. Vanessa suggested the possibility of an exhibition of the story of the project at the Scottish Parliament.

There will be an archive of the posters kept at Collective. Tom and Joanne might make a publication of the documentation of the project.

The Artists' working title is 'A direct experience in local time'. The group suggested 'What's it all: a boot' and 'The cat and boot' — like a public house.

The schools workshops will introduce ideas of public art and will be in the run up to the installation. There will be at least one off-site workshop for each of the school groups at either Robert Smails Press or with Edwin and Emlyn at Glasgow School of Art. Tom and Joanne will speak at one of the workshops.

PARTICIPATION

There will be workshops for the wider community most likely to be held in Inverleith Park. Debi is looking into the possibility of having the pedal powered cinema for one session. The theme will be public art but with different speakers and different experiences for each session.

Callum has given Geraldine and Debi notes of the Inverleith summer programme planning meeting dates. Someone will try to attend to get dates secured for the wider participation workshops.

SUMMER SCHOOL AND SYMPOSIUM

Debi and Kate gave a brief overview. Summer School will be for an audience with an active interest or background in contemporary art. This will be the only part of the project that it will cost to be involved in and will include trips to Jupiter Art Land and Little Sparta. The location for the Summer School is still to be confirmed. There might be a possibility of using a space at Broughton High School. Symposium on the Friday.

PUBLICITY

There will be an initial focus on the local area that will grow as the project develops. The posters will become more and more prominent in the area as the date of the opening approaches. Details will be in the Fringe Festival programme. Geraldine has started a blog on the Public Art Scotland website.

Many thanks to everyone for attending and participating in the discussions.

Next meeting Wednesday, 27 April 2011.

Glasgow, 29 October 2010

A conversation overheard in the foyer of the
Centre for Contemporary Arts.

THE ARCHITECT
Why do you think the Artists have called their
exhibition 'Direct serious action is therefore
necessary'?
THE INTERN
The title can be read as a provocative,
confrontational or instructional statement. It
seems to be saying, 'Listen, I have a message
for you.' The title appears to be constructed in a
way that allows it to directly address a viewer.
The Artists haven't chosen a title that describes or
labels the objects in the exhibition, and in fact the
title seems to have something of a problematic
relationship with these things. The phrase 'Direct
serious action is therefore necessary' does not
acknowledge the separate elements that make
up the exhibition; it doesn't obviously refer to or
describe a collection of objects, instead it states
a position or an attitude. There is no easy literal
connection between the artwork and the title …
This creates a problem or question that is central,
I think, to the exhibition. The question is this,
'What are these things in the CCA, why are they
here and what does it mean that they are here?'

THE ARCHITECT

How do you begin to answer those questions? In particular, I wonder what you think about the relationship between the different elements. There are the two large worm-like sculptures that occupy the cafe, foyer and galleries and then there are the black and white photographs of Glasgow ...

THE INTERN

Well, I think it's useful to understand both the worms and the photographs as interventions into the organisational and architectural context of the CCA, with the worms creating a sculptural disruption of the ground floor spaces and the photographs providing a more well-behaved counterpoint. However, while both these elements function as some sort of positioned intervention, if I then start to think more particularly about the subject matter of the sculptures and the photographs, the connection is disrupted. The subject matter of the photographs — Glasgow — doesn't seem to have a particular relationship to the worm sculptures, or for that matter to the exhibition title or the motif of a man on a horse. The Artists seem to be deliberately setting up relationships that undermine certain ways of accessing or interpreting the pieces.

THE ARCHITECT

So, why do you think the Artists chose to take photographs of Glasgow? Could the photographs be of anywhere?

THE INTERN

No, I think it matters that the photographs are here in Glasgow, but I think the Artists are using Glasgow as a trope — it stands in for the idea of subject matter. However, they have chosen something that has a particular significance within the context of the CCA — the photographs are being exhibited in Glasgow and are of Glasgow by artists who live in Glasgow. So, I think the fact of this makes it harder to overlook the literal meaning of the pictures — you cannot overlook the fact of Glasgow. There is a persuasive reading of the work that sees the photographs as representations of the artists' subjective encounter with the city they live in. Then you notice that a number of the images are repeated or appear to be repeated. The repetition reiterates the object quality of the photographs in their handmade frames. This draws you back to the presentation in the gallery and the processes of curation, of selection and positioning that seem to be central to this project.

THE ARCHITECT

Do you think that the large sculptures in the cafe and galleries have a similar relationship to their subject matter?

THE INTERN

Yes, I think there is a similar oscillation between what they are (giant worms!) and how they look and what they mean. The worms contain a number of contradictions within their formal structure. At first sight, the tail and hoops of the worm may appear to be painted abstract sculptures and the information that 'joins up' these pieces into the form of a worm arrives later with the appearance of the face. The face confirms the subject matter of the piece, whilst simultaneously undermining its status as a certain kind of sculpture. The cut out face makes the worm peculiarly active; it shifts the status of the work from a passive thing to be looked at, to something that looks back at the viewer — albeit illusionistically. The subject matter of worms has no immediately apparent resonance with the context of the CCA, but what it does do is draw attention to this context. Most apparently, the worm draws attention to the architecture of the CCA, and in doing so it allows a viewer to consider not only how the architecture provides a space within which the arts centre can conduct its activities, but also how the building becomes in fact a representation of such an organisation … The worm inevitably also offers scope for a more symbolic interpretation. The worm — or serpent — is the imaginary alien or other that in this instance stares aghast at the surroundings it now finds itself within.

THE ARCHITECT

The exhibition is accompanied by a text printed
in a leaflet that also features the man and
horse motif. Does this add anything to your
understanding of the work?

THE INTERN

Well, the text in the leaflet does seem to have
some correspondence with the photographs in
that it is of, or refers to Glasgow. The text draws
on an idiomatic and vernacular use of language
that is identifiably Glaswegian in its construction
and conventions. It's really a piece of prose that's
as much about its form as its subject matter —
but one in which the subject matter continues to
jostle for centre-stage. In this sense there is a
correspondence with the way the other elements
in the exhibition function. The text provides
an analogy for the artwork, rather than an
explanation.

THE ARCHITECT

A lot of your answers imply a process of
interpretation that is somewhat circular ... I get a
sense of the viewer being continuously redirected
from one potential point of meaning to another.

THE INTERN

I think you're right, I think this does happen
and it's through this process that the exhibition
functions. I think that the elements of the

exhibition are intended to encourage an active thinking about the codes and conventions of exhibition and the institutions that present them. The exhibition generates exchanges between the objects placed within the CCA and the context of the CCA itself and this is inevitably a somewhat circular process. This got me thinking about the idea of Ouroboros — the worm that eats itself. Ouroboros is a symbol of both self-reflexivity and cyclicality and I like the way this allows for a glimmer of an idea that the worms could almost be a symbol for how the exhibition functions! Ultimately, I think such a symbolic interpretation would be absurd, but it demonstrates how aspects of the exhibition shift across different models and systems of interpretation and have different points of access for a viewer. The title can be read as a provocative, confrontational or instructional statement. It seems to be saying, 'Listen, I have a message for you.'

Edinburgh, 28 August 2011

A volunteer leads a tour of the Fettes College grounds.

AT THE COLLEGE STEPS

Welcome to Fettes College. Fettes College is a leading co-educational boarding and day school for children aged thirteen to eighteen. The College is uniquely situated in extensive grounds and woodland close to the heart of Edinburgh, and enjoys a reputation for excellent academic results, the highest level of pastoral care, and a proud sporting tradition. It is perhaps best known as the school attended by New Labour Prime Minister Tony Blair. I'm going to lead a short tour of the immediate grounds of the College building and give you a brief history of the College. The tour will last about fifteen minutes, if you could now follow me and please make sure that you keep together as a group.

AT THE WEST CORNER OF THE CAR PARK

From here we can get a good view of the College building and beyond that we can see one of the Fettes' tennis courts and the new sports centre. Behind the College are the main playing fields and down towards the main entrance you came in at, at the edges of the Fettes grounds, are four of the College boarding houses – Glencourse, Moredun, Carrington and Kimmerghame. Fettes College was founded by Sir William Fettes. He was born in 1750 and began his working life at the age of 18 as a grocer. His business flourished and during the Napoleonic Wars he was contracted to provide provisions for troops stationed in Scotland. His wealth increased, as did his public status and he became Lord Provost of Edinburgh in 1800 and 1801. In 1804 he was made a Baronet. Sir William invested his wealth in property and land. He bought landed estates, which he then managed and let. In 1800 he purchased Comely Bank Estate, which was later to become the site of Fettes College. The death of his only son in 1815 meant that Sir William had no heir to leave his fortune to and so he established The Fettes Endowment for the Education, Maintenance and Outfit of Young People. If you could follow me now please.

AT THE HEADMASTER'S GARDEN

We're now standing in the Headmaster's Garden. If we look back the way we came we can see the Headmaster's Lodge. The current headmaster, Michael Spens, was educated at Marlborough and Selwyn College, Cambridge and is only the ninth headmaster at Fettes since it opened in 1870. When William Fettes died in 1836 his will stated that, 'The residue of my whole estate should form an Endowment for the maintenance, education and outfit of young people whose parents have either died without leaving sufficient funds for that purpose, or who, from innocent misfortune during their lives, are unable to give suitable education to their children.' However there was concern amongst the Trustees of the Endowment about the need and value of another such charitable hospital in Edinburgh. Benefactors such as George Herriot, George Watson and Daniel Stewart had set up hospitals, however the Endowed Schools Commission reported that such institutions were producing children who were dishonest, selfish and intellectually inert. The Fettes Trustees waited until the 1860s, watching Sir William's properties and the potential Endowment Trust grow in value. These 25 years also saw a shift in the focus of the Endowment. In 1862, the Trustees minutes record that the proposed institution might take the form of a 'Fettes College', rather than a charitable hospital. In 1872, following the Argyll Commission's condemnation of these hospitals, an Act was passed to turn them into fee-paying schools. This prepared the way for such institutions, as well as Fettes College, to become day schools for the middle classes. We'll now leave the garden and walk towards west side of the Chapel.

AT THE WEST SIDE OF THE CHAPEL
From here we have a good view of the exterior architecture of the Fettes College Chapel. The Chapel is an integral part of College life and all pupils attend the service that begins each day at Fettes. Each boarding house takes a turn at leading services for one week each term. The architect William Playfair was originally asked to design the building. Playfair had designed many of Edinburgh's landmark neo-classical buildings, including the National Gallery of Scotland and the unfinished National monument on Calton Hill. However, when Playfair died in 1857, the job went to his rival David Bryce. Bryce worked in what was to become known as the Scottish Baronial style and was designed to impress, using intricacy and flamboyance to make an architectural statement. This can be seen in the elaborate tracery and pinnacles of the College building and in the details such as the gargoyle water spouts. Fettes College was Bryce's masterpiece, however the extravagant external ornamentation came at a cost. Although William Fettes' original Endowment of £166,000 had risen to £484,000 by the time building began in 1864, the cost of the building

had also increased from £80,000 to nearly £140,000. This, combined with the high salary levels fixed by the Trustees, made it necessary for Fettes to become a fee-paying school. Edinburgh, with its high proportion of fee-paying educational establishments, presents ample opportunity to compare the minutiae that distinguish its schools. In the 1980s a Fettes master wrote, '...only a native (of Edinburgh) could possibly understand the complexities of status accorded to the various types of secondary school.' We'll now walk across to the far side of the car park, thank you.

AT THE EAST CORNER OF THE CAR PARK
From here we can look down towards the line of trees that marks the Green Walk that we walked past earlier. Although the Fettes grounds are extensive, they have shrunk in size over the years, sometimes in accordance with the wishes of the Fettes Governors and sometimes not. In the 1960s Edinburgh City Development plan earmarked 18 acres at the northwest corner as a site for Telford Technical College and another 14 acres were sold, under pressure, as a site for the new Police Headquarters. Also in the 1960s, the City of Edinburgh issued a compulsory purchase order for a further 15 acres as a site for the new Broughton High School. Fettes contested this

order, however at a Public Enquiry at the City Chambers in April 1963 the appeal was turned down and the enquiry concluded that a tenth of an acre per boy was 'as much as a Public School can expect to have these days when it has the misfortune of being situated within the confines of a large city.' If you could now follow me across to the lawned area by the College building.

BY THE QUEEN'S LAWN
We are now standing at the corner of Queen's Lawn, so called because it was laid to commemorate the visit of the Queen and Duke of Edinburgh to Fettes in 1955. Today one of the privileges of being a College prefect is to be allowed to walk across the lawn. Avoiding the lawn, if we could now make our way over to the War Memorial.

AT THE WAR MEMORIAL
The Fettes War Memorial was built in 1921 from a design by Burnie Rhind to commemorate Fettesians who have fallen in war. It is the annual setting for Remembrance Sunday Services and marks the parade ground for the College's combined cadet force. The cadet force, with links to all three armed forces, is a strong tradition at Fettes and there is a strong emphasis on extra-

curricular activities such as mountaineering and piping. The idea of leadership is of course central to the Fettes ethos, with the website stating that 'the understanding of and preparation for leadership are built into a pupil's development at all levels'. Current fees stand at £8,620 per term for the senior school and there is an incentive for further family members to attend with a 5% reduction for a second child, 35% for a third and 50% for any subsequent children. Sir William's original wishes are today covered by the provision of scholarships that pay up to 10% of the fees for excellence in areas including piping, sports and music. Scholarship holders are also eligible to apply for a means tested bursary that would then account for 95% of the fees.

The experience
being an experience
like an experience
you just had

A proposal for the 2012 Cultural
Olympiad: submitted 9 October
2009 and presented to the Artists
Taking the Lead selection panel
19 October 2009

An unsuccessful proposal
for the 2012
Cultural Olympiad
(The experience
being an experience
like an experience
you just had)

Four framed drawings,
each 53 × 66cm, illustrations
by Simon Manfield

Does your contemplation
of the situation
fuck with
the flow of circulation

Eastside Projects, Birmingham
4 July to 6 September 2009

Two billboard posters: digital
prints, each 305 × 610cm

Wall painting with five posters:
paint, digital prints, 400 ×
1680cm

Tunnel: MDF, timber, paint,
245 × 760 × 1090cm

Digital projection: duration
4 minutes, 50 seconds in a
continuous loop

The tunnel remained at
Eastside Projects for two further
exhibitions:

'Abstract Cabinet Show',
26 September to 8 November
2009

'Two Short Plays by Liam Gillick',
27 November to 23 January
2010

Invitation card: printed offset,
die cut circle, designed with
James Langdon

Exhibition publication:
newsprint, 24 pages, designed
with James Langdon

Talks and events: scripted
presentation and exhibition tour
for Birmingham Institute of Art
and Design fine art staff, 8 July
2009; scripted presentation with
Gavin Wade, 3 September 2009;
scripted presentation, Eastside
Projects 'Public Evaluation
Event', 29 October 2011

Eastside Projects print edition:
diptych, silkscreen on paper, 42
× 59.4cm, edition of 20

Photography by Stuart Whipps,
pages 119 to 123

Direct serious action
is therefore necessary

Centre for Contemporary Arts,
Glasgow
2 October to 13 November 2010

Worm constructions: MDF,
timber, paint, dimensions
variable

16 black and white photographs
in hand-made frames; Untitled
(Westburn Bar); Untitled
(Hunterian Gallery); Untitled
(Cawder Cuilt); Untitled
(Financial Services Office);
Untitled (Horslethill Road);
Untitled (Notre Dame); Untitled
(Cranhill land); Untitled (The
Castle); Untitled (Forth and
Clyde); Untitled (Notre Dame);
Untitled (Lanark Street); Untitled
(Tramway); Untitled (Westburn
Bar); Untitled (Kelvinside
Terrace); Untitled (Airlink);
Untitled (Jewsons): plywood,
glass, beeswax, brass mirror
plates, each 60.5 × 72.5 × 6.5cm

Painted panels from the worm
structures were re-used by CCA
at their Westhorn allotment in
Glasgow's East End

Invitation card: printed offset,
cartoon motif and text by Joanne
Tatham & Tom O'Sullivan,
designed with Sarah Tripp

Interpretation leaflet: Question
and answer text by Joanne
Tatham & Tom O'Sullivan,
photocopied folded A4 leaflet

Talks and events: a tour of the
CCA building with architect Ewan
Imrie and CCA house manager
Alasdair Rothin, 13 November
2010; Gavin Wade in discussion
with Francis McKee, 26 October
2010; screening of 'Incident at
Loch Ness', by Werner Herzog
and Zak Penn, 15 October 2010

Photography by Ruth Clark,
pages 113 to 118

The indirect exchange
of uncertain value

Collective off-site project at
Fettes College, Edinburgh
5 to 28 August 2011

Visitors to The indirect exchange
of uncertain value were given a
thirty-minute scripted tour of the
Fettes College grounds

Boot: plywood, steel frame, paint,
timber door, sound proofing
material, 340 × 500 × 200cm

Cat: plywood, steel frame,
paint, timber door, vinyl flooring,
590 × 710 × 150cm

Inside the boot: CHOIR (2011)
by Elizabeth Price, HD video,
duration 10 minutes

Inside the cat: Portrait of a
Recipient as a Door Handle,
After a Drawing Produced by
an Anonymous Philanthropist,
Bronze Maquette, Scale 3:2
(2010) by Chris Evans, bronze
maquette, 15 × 25 × 111 cm

Inside Fettes College Callover
hall: NEW RULES 4 (2011) by
Chris Evans, bronze with ivory
patina, 48 × 1.2 cm

Symposium
5 August 2011, presentations by
Vito Acconci, Chris Evans,
Owen Hatherley, Fiona Jardine,
Tom Leonard and Elizabeth Price

Participation programme,
devised and co-ordinated by
Debi Bannerjee: Public Art
Summer School, 1 to 5 August
2011; workshops for pupils from
Fettes College and Broughton
High School

Steering group: Jack Bannerman
(Stockbridge and Inverleith
Community Council), Barbara
Conway (Fettes College),
Pauline Cumming (Broughton
High School), Vanessa
Glynn (Stockbridge resident),
Gemma Gray (Fettes College),
Elaine Lennon (Inverleith
Neighbourhood Partnership),
Callum Macleod (Inverleith
Community Learning and
Development Officer)

Invitation card and project
posters: 14 posters by the artists,
Fettes College / Broughton High
School pupils and symposium
participants, letterpress and
offset, designed by Edwin
Pickstone and Emlyn Firth

Collective project guide with
essay by Fiona Jardine

Photography by Ruth Clark,
pages 124 to 128

Joanne Tatham and Tom O'Sullivan would like to thank the following people and organisations for their support in the making of the work and this publication

Kitty Anderson, Debi Bannerjee, Tom Bloor, Jill Brown, Ruth Clark, Barbara Conway, Alan Dimmick, Chris Dyson, Chris Evans, Emlyn Firth, Belinda Gilbert Scott, Gemma Gray, Kate Gray, Andrew Hamilton, Geraldine Heany, Simon Hopkins, Ewan Imrie, Fiona Jardine, Alan Kean, Rob Kennedy, Jamie Kenyon, Robin Kirkham, James Langdon, Francis McKee, Simon Manfield, Rory Middleton, Kerri Moogan, Neil Mulholland, Katie Nicol, Edwin Pickstone, Elizabeth Price, Jenny Richards, Alasdair Rothin, Sarah Tripp, Lesley Young, Gavin Wade, Stuart Whipps, Toby Webster, Jess Worrall

The Modern Institute/ Toby Webster Ltd, Glasgow; Eastside Projects, Birmingham; CCA, Glasgow; Collective, Edinburgh; Fettes College, Edinburgh; Collective Architecture, Glasgow; Scottish Arts Council / Creative Scotland; Henry Moore Foundation; The Elephant Trust; Northumbria University

A special thank you to all the members of the technical teams who helped construct, paint and install the work

Amongst other things
an unsuccessful proposal
for the 2012
Cultural Olympiad

Edited by
Joanne Tatham & Tom O'Sullivan
with James Langdon

Text by Joanne Tatham
and Tom O'Sullivan

Additional texts:

Page 7, from 'Artists taking the
lead' press release

Pages 9 to 10, by Gavin Wade,
'Eastside Project User's Manual'

Pages 11 to 12, by Francis
McKee, 'Arts Professional'
magazine

Designed by James Langdon
with
Joanne Tatham & Tom O'Sullivan

Typeface by An Endless Supply

Published in an edition of 1000
in 2012

Distributed by

Cornerhouse Publications
70 Oxford Street
Manchester M1 5NH

Tel. +44 (0) 161 200 1503
www.cornerhouse.org/books

Centre for Contemporary Arts
350 Sauchiehall Street
Glasgow G2 3JD

Tel. +44 (0) 141 352 4900
www.cca-glasgow.com

CCA is a company guaranteed
with charitable status. Registered
company number: SC140944.
Registered Scottish Charity
number: SC020734. CCA is
supported by Creative Scotland
and Glasgow Life. We are
grateful for the financial support
of The Modern Institute and
Eastside Projects, Birmingham in
producing this publication.

Eastside Projects
86 Heath Mill Lane
Birmingham B9 4AR

Tel. +44 (0)121 771 1778
www.eastsideprojects.org

Eastside Projects is a not for
profit company Limited by
guarantee 6402007, an Arts
Council England National
Portfolio Organisation in
partnership with Birmingham
City University, supported
by Paul Hamlyn Foundation
Breakthrough Fund.

CCA:
Centre for
Contemporary Arts

**Eastside
Projects**

ALBA | CHRUTHACHAIL

118

123